A Note from Mary Pope Osborne and Natalie Pope Boyce About Magic Tree House® Fact Tracker: *World War II*

Dear Parents and Teachers,

When Magic Tree House Super Edition #1: *Danger in the Darkest Hour* (now called *World at War, 1944*) first came out, we did not plan to write a nonfiction Fact Tracker companion. In the super edition, Jack and Annie parachute into France during World War II to help the French Resistance. Since World War II was the deadliest war in history, we were concerned that a factual account might be too advanced a subject for young readers.

We changed our minds, however, because we've had many requests for such a book. It's our hope that we've handled the material in a sensitive but truthful manner and that young readers will get a basic introduction to this vitally important period in world history.

If children have questions about World War II, the books and websites listed in the Doing More Research section in the back of this book can be helpful. If they have questions about the Holocaust chapter, the United States Holocaust Memorial Museum's website, ushmm.org, has information and resources that can aid your conversations.

Many thanks,

Mary Pope Osborne   Natalie Pope Boyce

Here's what kids, parents, and teachers have to say about the Magic Tree House® Fact Trackers:

"They are so good. I can't wait for the next one. All I can say for now is prepare to be amazed!" —Alexander N.

"I have read every Magic Tree House book there is. The [Fact Trackers] are a thrilling way to get more information about the special events in the story." —John R.

"These are fascinating nonfiction books that enhance the magical time-traveling adventures of Jack and Annie. I love these books, especially *American Revolution.* I was learning so much, and I didn't even know it!" —Tori Beth S.

"[They] are an excellent 'behind-the-scenes' look at what the [Magic Tree House fiction] has started in your imagination! You can't buy one without the other; they are such a complement to one another." —Erika N., mom

"Magic Tree House [Fact Trackers] took my children on a journey from Frog Creek, Pennsylvania, to so many significant historical events! The detailed manuals are a remarkable addition to the classic fiction Magic Tree House books we adore!" —Jenny S., mom

"[They] are very useful tools in my classroom, as they allow for students to be part of the planning process. Together, we find facts in the [Fact Trackers] to extend the learning introduced in the fictional companions. Researching and planning classroom activities, such as our class Olympics based on facts found in *Ancient Greece and the Olympics,* help create a genuine love for learning!" —Paula H., teacher

Magic Tree House®
Fact Tracker

WORLD WAR II

A nonfiction companion to
Magic Tree House® Super Edition #1:
World at War, 1944

by Mary Pope Osborne
and Natalie Pope Boyce

illustrated by Carlo Molinari

A STEPPING STONE BOOK™
Random House 🏠 New York

Text copyright © 2017 by Mary Pope Osborne and Natalie Pope Boyce
Interior illustrations copyright © 2017 by Penguin Random House LLC
Cover photograph copyright © by Print Collector/Getty Images

The Magic Tree House Fact Tracker series was formerly known as the Magic
Tree House Research Guide series. *World at War, 1944* was previously
published in hardcover as *Danger in the Darkest Hour.*

Visit us on the Web!
SteppingStonesBooks.com
MagicTreeHouse.com

Educators and librarians, for a variety of teaching tools, visit us at
RHTeachersLibrarians.com

Library of Congress Cataloging-in-Publication Data
Names: Osborne, Mary Pope, author. | Boyce, Natalie Pope, author. | Molinari,
Carlo, illustrator.
Title: World War II / by Mary Pope Osborne and Natalie Pope Boyce ;
illustrated by Carlo Molinari.
Description: First edition. | New York : Random House, 2017. | Series: Magic
Tree House Fact Tracker ; 36 | "A nonfiction companion to Magic Tree House
Super Edition #1 : World at War, 1944." | "A Stepping Stone Book." |
Identifiers: LCCN 2016037491 | ISBN 978-1-101-93639-9 (trade pbk.) |
ISBN 978-1-101-93640-5 (hardcover library binding) |
ISBN 978-1-101-93641-2 (ebook)
Subjects: LCSH: World War, 1939–1945—Juvenile literature.
Classification: LCC D743.7 .O69 2017 | DDC 940.53—dc23

Printed in the United States of America

10 9 8 7 6 5 4 3 2 1

This book has been officially leveled by using the F&P Text Level Gradient™
Leveling System.

Dedicated to Second Lieutenant Robert A. Johnson and all the men of the Eighth Air Force with whom he served in World War II

Grateful acknowledgment to Jeremy Greensmith, fifth-grade teacher, PS 321, Brooklyn, and Rena Zurofsky for their helpful reading of this book.

Historical Consultant:
MICHAEL NEIBERG, professor of history, Department of National Security Studies, U.S. Army War College

Education Consultant:
HEIDI JOHNSON, language acquisition and science education specialist, Bisbee, Arizona

Special thanks to the excellent staff at Random House: Mallory Loehr, Paula Sadler, Jenna Lettice, Heather Palisi, Jason Zamajtuk, Carlo Molinari for the great art, and especially to our superb editor, Diane Landolf

WORLD WAR II

Contents

Dear Readers,

This is our most serious Fact Tracker yet. Due to the subject matter, it is meant for older Magic Tree House readers. In <u>World at War, 1944</u>, we parachuted behind enemy lines in Normandy, France, to help defeat the Nazis. Many countries fought in World War II, and millions of people died. Whole cities were destroyed.

We needed to know more about it. How did it begin? Why did Germany and Japan start the fighting? We wanted the facts, even though the facts are difficult to take.

As usual, we got out our notebooks and went to work. The Internet helped us, but we also read a lot of books. There is so much information out there about World War II that it wasn't very hard to get answers to our questions.

We want to share our research with you. So strap on your parachutes, and let's hit the ground to learn all about World War II.

Jack

Annie

1

World War II

World War II began in 1939 and lasted for six long years. More people died in this war than in any other war in history. When it was over, at least 50 million people had been killed. Millions had suffered serious injuries. And after years of bombing, cities lay in ruins, leaving millions of people homeless.

Altogether, sixty-one countries and 100

13

million soldiers took part in the war. Most of the fighting was in Europe, North Africa, and Asia. There were battles on land, in the sky, and on the sea.

Choosing Sides

Germany, Italy, and Japan were the major countries in a group called the *Axis* powers. Countries belonging to the Axis wanted to gain power by taking over other countries.

Great Britain, France, the *Soviet Union*, the United States, and China joined together against the Axis. These countries were called the *Allies*.

Germany After World War I

In 1918, the Germans lost World War I, along with Austria-Hungary and the

Ottoman Empire. They had fought against Britain, France, Italy, Russia, Japan, and the United States.

Kaiser Wilhelm II, the last emperor of Germany, who ruled during World War I, had to live in the Netherlands after the war.

The French and British thought that Germany caused the war. As punishment, the Germans had to sign a strict peace treaty called the Treaty of Versailles (ver-SIGH). The treaty said that Germany could only have a small army and navy and had to give up many of its territories.

Signing the Treaty of Versailles

The treaty made the Germans accept blame for World War I. It also said they had to pay for damages the war had caused. Being forced to sign the treaty left many Germans angry and ashamed.

Rise of Adolf Hitler

As time passed, a lot of Germans who thought losing the war was not the German Army's fault came to believe that a man named Adolf Hitler could help Germany become a powerful country.

Hitler urged the Germans to fight to destroy the treaty. "Germany awake!" he would shout as thousands cheered.

Hitler was a very dangerous man with dangerous ideas. He claimed that the Germans were the master race who should rule all of Europe. The Europe he wanted to create had no place for Jews, Slavs—a group of people from Eastern European countries including Poland and what was then Yugoslavia—and others who he claimed were not true Germans.

Hitler Comes to Power

Political parties are groups of people who share the same ideas about how governments should work. In 1921, Hitler became the head of a new political party called the Nazi party.

The Nazi salute was called the <u>Sieg Heil</u>, which means "Hail, victory!"

Adolf Hilter

The Nazis put an ancient symbol called a <u>swastika</u> on their flags and uniforms.

Hitler and the other Nazis believed that one strong leader should rule Germany. They also shared a deep, unforgivable hatred for Jewish people. Although it wasn't true, they blamed Jews for Germany's defeat in the First World War.

In 1934, the Germans elected Hitler as president of Germany. Hitler quickly turned into a brutal *dictator* who used force to get his way.

A dictator is a <u>ruler who has</u> all the power in the government.

19

Members of the Gestapo didn't have to obey the laws, and no one could stop what they were doing.

The Secret State Police, called the *Gestapo,* watched carefully to discover if anyone was working against the Nazis. Whenever people spoke out, they were killed or put in jail. Many Germans, especially those who were Jewish, chose to flee Germany to live in other countries. The famous physicist Albert Einstein was one of them.

Invasion of Poland

In 1939, Hitler began his plan to take over Europe by invading Poland in a

blitzkrieg (BLITZ-kreeg) attack. The invasion happened so suddenly that other countries couldn't stop it.

Britain and France immediately declared war on Germany. World War II had begun. Two years later, the United States joined the fight.

Blitzkrieg means "lightning war" in German. German soldiers were trained to fight short, very violent battles.

Germany Invades Other Countries

After Poland, the Germans invaded Norway, Denmark, France, the Netherlands, Belgium, Greece, Yugoslavia, and the Soviet Union.

Nazis flew their flag from the Eiffel Tower.

China

Japan

Pacific Ocean

War in the Pacific

Japan is a chain of islands in the Pacific Ocean. The country doesn't have many natural resources like oil, coal, rubber, and copper. In order to build up its wealth and power, Japan looked to seize these things from other countries.

The emperor of Japan was named Hirohito. Hideki Tojo was his powerful prime minister. Their plan was to control Southeast Asia and the Pacific. Then Japan could take natural resources from the countries it conquered.

In 1937, the Japanese began the war in the Pacific by invading China. Their attack was so brutal that millions of Chinese died. Chiang Kai-shek, who led China, had well-trained soldiers, but they couldn't stop the Japanese invasion.

Japanese troops march into Kaifeng, China, during the invasion in 1938.

Three years later, Japan signed a pact with Germany and Italy and joined forces with the Axis.

Bombing of Pearl Harbor

Oil is necessary to run factories and machinery.

To try to stop Japan, warships in the U.S. Pacific Fleet refused to let ships from other countries deliver oil to Japan.

In 1941, Tojo ordered Japanese naval aircraft to attack the U.S. Pacific Fleet in Pearl Harbor, Hawaii. His goal was to destroy U.S. naval ships anchored in the harbor.

U.S. fighter planes destroyed

Early on the morning of December 7, two waves of Japanese fighter planes swooped down on Pearl Harbor.

Some dropped bombs and torpedoes, blowing up ships in the harbor. Others attacked U.S. fighter planes on the ground so they couldn't take off to defend the ships.

A total of nineteen ships were destroyed, and 2,403 sailors lost their lives.

The surprise attack left a mass of burning, mangled ships and many dead and injured sailors. The largest ship lost was the aircraft carrier U.S.S. *Arizona*, along with more than 1,100 of its sailors.

The U.S.S. <u>West Virginia</u> was also attacked.

Declaring War

Until then, the United States had not entered the war. The day after Pearl Harbor, Franklin Roosevelt, president of the United States, asked Congress to declare war on Japan.

In the Second World War, most people got their news from radios. There were very few TVs.

As Americans huddled around their radios, the president's voice filled their living rooms with the grim news.

A few days later, Germany declared war on the United States, and this is when the United States joined the Allies.

Getting Ready

By 1940, America was building airplanes, tanks, ships, submarines, and weapons to sell to the Allies. After the United States joined the war, factories began making these things for American soldiers as well.

President Roosevelt said that every man, woman, and child in America should be partners in fighting the war. Because so many men went away to war, women who had never worked before took jobs in factories.

"I WANT <u>YOU</u> IN THE NAVY and I WANT YOU <u>NOW</u>"

By the time the war ended, the United States had built more than 300,000 planes, 90,000 tanks, and 200 submarines.

Soldiers

After war was declared, people hurried to join the fight. Since there still weren't enough soldiers, the government made a

rule that men from the ages of eighteen to forty-five could be *drafted* to fight for their country.

Over 16 million American soldiers took part in the war. Many were away from home for a year or more. Overnight, life in the United States had completely changed.

To be <u>drafted</u> means to be ordered to join the military when the country needs soldiers.

Military Timeline for World War II

1939   1940   1941

Germany invades Poland. Britain and France declare war on Germany.

Germany invades the Soviet Union. Japan attacks Pearl Harbor, and the United States enters the war against Japan and Germany.

Germany invades Norway, Denmark, France, Belgium, and the Netherlands. Germans bomb Britain. Japan and Italy join the Axis.

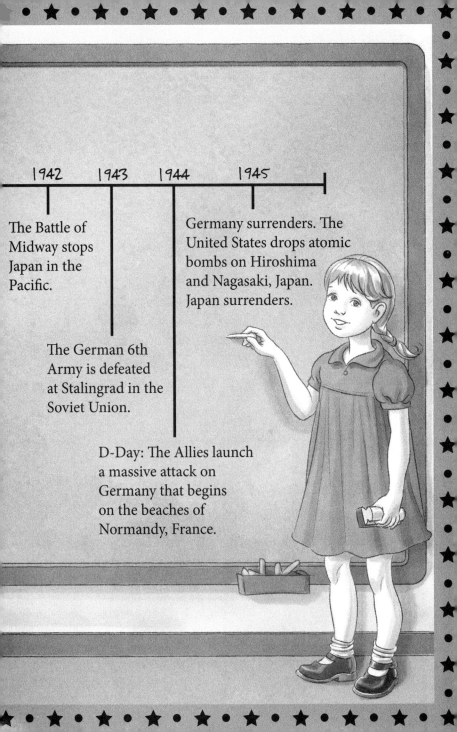

| 1942 | 1943 | 1944 | 1945 |

The Battle of Midway stops Japan in the Pacific.

Germany surrenders. The United States drops atomic bombs on Hiroshima and Nagasaki, Japan. Japan surrenders.

The German 6th Army is defeated at Stalingrad in the Soviet Union.

D-Day: The Allies launch a massive attack on Germany that begins on the beaches of Normandy, France.

2

The Leaders

The leaders of the Allies and the Axis risked their countries' futures by entering the war. Four of the leaders would win. Three would lose everything, even their lives.

Franklin Delano Roosevelt of the United States, Joseph Stalin of the Soviet Union, Winston Churchill of Great Britain, and Chiang Kai-shek of China led the Allies.

Churchill, Roosevelt, and Stalin were known as the Big Three. They met during the war to plan how the Allies could win.

Winston Churchill and Franklin Roosevelt were great leaders who guided their countries well.

Joseph Stalin joined the Allies when Germany attacked the Soviet Union. He was a harsh dictator who forced people to do what he wanted. Stalin killed millions of his people by starving them or putting them in labor camps.

The leaders of the Axis were Adolf Hitler of Germany, Benito Mussolini of Italy, and Hideki Tojo of Japan.

As head of the Nazi party and leader of Germany, Hitler was responsible for starting World War II.

Benito Mussolini was a *fascist* (FA-shist) who dreamed of Italy becoming as powerful as it had once been during the Roman Empire.

Fascists believe in a strong leader who completely controls the people.

Mussolini's brutal supporters were known as the Blackshirts because of the black uniform shirts they wore.

Benito Mussolini

Hirohito was emperor of Japan. Hideki Tojo was his prime minister. Tojo was a high-ranking general who thought that the Japanese were a superior people. He believed they had the right to rule Southeast Asia.

Hideki Tojo

Tojo helped create a well-trained military in which soldiers obeyed without question and believed it was an honor to die in battle.

Italy and Japan Join the Axis
Mussolini, Hitler, and Tojo all believed they had the right to make their own

countries stronger by taking over other countries.

Mussolini invaded the African country of Ethiopia in 1935.

The Ethiopians fought hard but couldn't defeat the Italians.

Between 1940 and 1941, Italy tried to take over Greece. That plan failed, and the Germans occupied Greece instead.

Mussolini knew he needed Hitler's help and joined the Axis.

Because the United States and Britain were against Japan's attempt to conquer other nations, Tojo saw them as enemies. In 1940, he joined the Axis and signed an agreement to support Germany and Italy.

Stalin Joins the Allies
The Soviet Union and Germany were on the same side at the beginning of the war. But in 1941, Hitler shocked Stalin by invading the Soviet Union. Stalin had no choice but to join Britain in the fight against Germany.

Roosevelt Talks to the People
Franklin Delano Roosevelt was the thirty-second president of the United States. He

was popular, and people often called him by his initials, FDR.

When Roosevelt was thirty-nine years old, he had a terrible disease called polio that paralyzed his legs. For the rest of his life, he needed to wear heavy metal braces and use crutches to walk.

Photographs of Roosevelt didn't show how disabled he was.

During the war, FDR often spoke on the radio. He called his talks fireside chats. For the first time in history, people could listen to a president tell them how things were going in the government and in the war.

President Roosevelt always began his talks by saying "My fellow Americans" or "My friends." Then he talked to them just as if he were in their living rooms. Most Americans felt that FDR really was their friend.

Churchill Inspires the British

Winston Churchill was born in a palace in England. In 1940, he became Britain's prime minister.

Winston Churchill

Winston Churchill was a brilliant writer and speaker. Like President Roosevelt, he spoke on the radio to give his people hope and strength.

In his most famous speech, Winston Churchill said, "We shall fight on the beaches, we shall fight on the landing grounds, we shall fight in the fields and in the streets, we shall fight in the hills. We shall never surrender."

Now let's meet the military leaders of World War II.

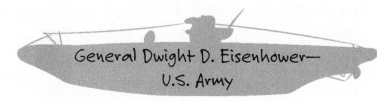
General Dwight D. Eisenhower—
U.S. Army

General Eisenhower grew up with six
brothers in a small Kansas town. After high
school, he worked for two years to pay for
his brother to go to college. In 1911, he left
home to study at West Point, the United
States Military Academy.

By the Second World War, Dwight
Eisenhower had become a general. He was
made supreme commander of the Allied
forces in Europe and was one of the main
planners of the D-Day invasion.

Before D-Day, Eisenhower put a note

in his pocket saying that if the invasion failed, it would be his fault.

After the war, General Eisenhower, whose nickname was Ike, was so popular, he became president of the United States in 1953 and served two terms.

Eisenhower (center) and other leaders camped in Portsmouth, England, as they planned the D-Day invasion.

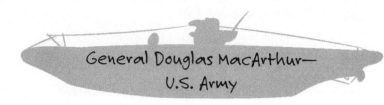
General Douglas MacArthur—
U.S. Army

General Douglas MacArthur was the son of a high-ranking army general. He said he learned to ride and shoot before he could read or write. General MacArthur and his father both won Congressional Medals of Honor.

Douglas MacArthur graduated from West Point at the top of his class. As a general, he was in charge of the war in the Pacific.

Though General MacArthur was some-times short of supplies and men and faced hard fighting, his forces managed to defeat the Japanese.

After the war, General MacArthur was in charge of rebuilding Japan. When he retired, he gave a famous speech to Congress and said, "Old soldiers never die; they just fade away."

MacArthur signed the Japanese surrender on September 2, 1945.

Field Marshal Bernard Montgomery—
British Army

Bernard Montgomery led the British defeat of the Axis in North Africa. He was also a major force in the D-Day invasion.

General Montgomery grew up on Tasmania, an Australian island where his Irish father was a minister. He was wounded and almost died during World War I.

In 1942, Montgomery—or Monty, as his men called him—planned the Second Battle of El Alamein, a turning point in North Africa. He became a hero, and crowds cheered him in the streets.

General Montgomery was made a field marshal, the highest rank in the British Army. Field Marshal Montgomery liked to argue, and although he and General Eisenhower sometimes disagreed, they managed to plan the D-Day invasion together.

3

On Land, in the Sky, and on the Sea

Airplanes played a huge part in the war. Heavy bombers took off from air bases to drop bombs on the enemy. Large transport planes risked danger by flying low over enemy lines to drop *paratroopers* to fight.

Paratroopers are soldiers who jump out of airplanes with parachutes.

Fighter planes were equipped with machine guns and cannons. To protect soldiers on the ground and to stop enemy bombing raids, they often had dogfights with enemy planes in the air. Dogfights are battles between fighter planes flying close to one another and firing machine guns.

Airplanes of World War II

 The Fairchild C-82 Packet was an American cargo plane also used to carry paratroopers.

A Dangerous Job

It was very dangerous to fly during the war: 18,000 American airmen were wounded, and 40,000 lost their lives.

Besides being dangerous, it was also

British Spitfires were the most famous planes in the war. They fought German Messerschmitts in the Battle of Britain.

Spitfires

Messerschmitts

uncomfortable. There was no heat in the planes. Some climbed up to 29,000 feet, where temperatures could dip to sixty degrees below zero Fahrenheit!

Airmen had to wear oxygen masks, steel helmets, and heavy gloves. They also wore a clip that could be hooked to a parachute in case they were shot down.

These members of the Eighth Air Force have just returned from a mission over Germany.

Ships and Submarines

German submarines were known as U-boats. One of their missions was to destroy Allied ships carrying supplies to the soldiers. So many supply ships were lost that they began to travel in groups called convoys. Warships traveled with the convoys to protect them.

For the first time, large aircraft carriers played a big part in a war. These huge ships were like floating runways. Their decks were large enough for

Most of the U.S. aircraft carriers were in the Pacific.

planes to take off and land. And they were filled with fuel for the planes.

Because the ships moved around, it was easy to get planes to places they wouldn't have had enough fuel to fly to. The aircraft carriers brought the planes close to where they were needed, and pilots took off right from the ships. After an airstrike or battle, pilots landed on their carriers, refueled, and flew out to fight again.

Tanks

Both the Allies and the Axis had tanks. The two most powerful German tanks were the

German Panzer tank

Panzer and Tiger tanks. The United States used Sherman tanks, which could be produced in greater numbers.

What Soldiers Carried

Unless they were in the middle of a fight, soldiers carried a lot of equipment around with them.

Training

New soldiers had to report to military bases for basic training. When they got there, military barbers shaved their heads. Then they were given uniforms, socks, and underwear.

The most important thing the men learned was to obey orders even though they might disagree with them.

Captain Benjamin O. Davis led the famous all-black group of fighter pilots known as the Tuskegee Airmen.

Tough drill sergeants trained the men. They usually yelled a lot until their men got things right. The drill sergeants kept the soldiers in shape by making them run, hike, march, and do push-ups.

The men also practiced hand-to-hand combat and firing weapons. When they left basic training, the soldiers were ready to fight.

Charge along with us to learn about some of the biggest battles of the war.

Battle of Britain, July–October 1940

After the invasion of Poland, the Germans began bombing air bases in Britain. The British fought back by bombing Berlin, the capital of Germany.

Hitler's bombing of British cities was called the Blitz.

Hitler was furious and ordered his pilots to bomb London and other major English cities.

Almost every night, air-raid sirens sounded warnings all across Britain to let people know that German planes were on the way. People dropped whatever they were doing and hurried to the nearest air-raid shelter.

During the Blitz, German planes bombed London for seventy-one days in a row.

Many of the bombs caused fires. Men ages sixteen to sixty were in charge of

Air-raid shelters were underground spaces like subway stations and basements in hospitals or schools that were safe from the bombs.

spotting and reporting the fires. Volunteer air-raid wardens, some of them women, rushed to help put them out.

Sixty thousand people died in the Blitz, and two million homes were destroyed. The bombings ended only when Hitler ordered his planes to turn away from Britain and attack Russia.

Battle of Stalingrad,
September 1942–February 1943

On July 9, 1942, Hitler ordered the invasion of the Soviet Union to begin. He especially wanted to take the city of Stalingrad, which was named for Joseph Stalin.

Stalingrad was a major port city with lots of factories. Capturing it would have given Hitler's armies a way to get to the Soviet Union's oil fields so they could cut off Stalin's fuel supply.

The Battle of Stalingrad lasted through the winter of 1942–1943. The Germans blocked all supplies like food or fuel from reaching people stranded in the city.

They were left to face the freezing winter without heat. Many were sick and starving, but they didn't give up.

General Georgy Zhukov was a brilliant soldier who won many victories for the Soviet Union. He ordered his soldiers to break into small groups and use the ruins of buildings for protection. The soldiers became street fighters who carried out surprise attacks.

General Zhukov

Women and children dug trenches and built barricades. Sometimes they even fought alongside Russian soldiers. Hand-to-hand combat was common. Soviet soldiers used the tunnels in the city's sewer system to sneak up on the invaders.

Finally Soviet soldiers were able to surround the Germans.

Like the people of Stalingrad, the Germans couldn't get warm clothes, boots, food, or weapons. In February, Germany gave up the fight for Stalingrad.

The Soviets took 91,000 German soldiers captive. Forty thousand citizens of Stalingrad had died. The Soviet Union lost over a million soldiers and the Axis over 850,000, but the Soviets had driven back the Nazi invaders.

Battle of Midway,
June 4–7, 1942

By 1942, Japan controlled most of Southeast Asia and much of the Pacific Ocean. There was a small U.S. naval base on Midway Island, halfway between Asia and North America.

The Japanese planned a sneak attack on the Americans. They worked out their plans in code. Code breakers in the United States figured out the code.

The naval commander, Admiral Chester W. Nimitz, sent three aircraft carriers to attack the four Japanese carriers headed to the base.

For four days, American dive-bombers from the carriers swooped down from high in the air to attack the ships. Because the Japanese didn't plan for an air attack, their carrier guns were aimed too low to fire back.

The Japanese lost their four aircraft carriers, plus 248 planes and 3,000 sailors. The Japanese defeat was a turning point for the Allies in the Pacific.

D-Day Invasion, June 1944

The Germans marched into France in 1940. In June 1944, 150,000 soldiers from

Britain, the United States, Canada, and France gathered in Britain to prepare for the biggest attack from the sea in history.

The Allies called the day of the attack D-Day. They'd been planning it for years.

On June 6, shortly after midnight, the attack began. The Allies had hoped

D-Day is a term the military sometimes uses for the day of a planned attack. The "D" doesn't stand for anything except "Day."

for a bright night because of the full moon, but it was cloudy. General Eisenhower decided to strike anyway.

First, paratroopers landed behind enemy lines in France to destroy bridges and cut off escape routes. To confuse the Germans, planes also dropped dummies that looked like men. They were filled with firecrackers.

Then bombers dropped bombs on the German lines. After that, 6,000 boats approached the Normandy beaches, bringing Allied tanks, weapons, and soldiers.

Fighting on the beaches was brutal. About 9,000 Allied soldiers were wounded or died during the invasion.

After D-Day, the Allies moved farther into France and began to force the Germans to retreat.

American soldiers march to block a German retreat in the Battle of the Bulge.

Battle of the Bulge, December 1944

December 16, 1944, was a cold day in the Ardennes forest in Belgium. Four divisions of exhausted American soldiers were camped in the woods to rest.

The Germans attacked with a force of 200,000 men and 1,000 tanks. Thousands of American soldiers died as the Germans pushed fifty miles through the American lines, creating a bulge in their defenses.

The Americans worked in small groups to attack the Germans and survive until more soldiers arrived to help.

The narrow icy roads, blizzards, and fog caused a fuel shortage for the German tanks. More American soldiers arrived to join the fight and keep up the attacks.

After five weeks of fierce fighting, the battle was over. Between 80,000 and 100,000 German soldiers lay dead. The Americans lost over 75,000 soldiers. Thousands more were wounded.

The Americans had won a hard victory, and Hitler's once-proud army was badly hurt.

During the battle, the Germans asked American General Anthony McAuliffe to surrender. He sent the Germans a famous message—his answer was "Nuts!" He didn't surrender.

4

The Home Front

As soldiers prepared to go to war, people at home got ready as well. Their biggest jobs were to be sure there were enough weapons, equipment, and food for the millions of soldiers overseas.

To remind people that the soldiers came first, the U.S. government made posters that said things like "Do with less so they'll have enough." Soldiers were depending on people at home for help.

People pitched in to aid the war effort. There were drives all over the country to collect and recycle scrap metal. It took 900 tons of metal just to make one large warship!

People, including schoolkids and community organizations, turned in piles of tin cans, rubber tires, scrap metal from cars, silk cloth, bottles, paper, and more. All these things were remade into useful materials for the soldiers.

The silk was for parachutes.

Ration Books

It was dangerous for ships to bring certain foods like sugar to the United States. And much of the food produced in America had to go to the soldiers. So there were food shortages.

Families had war *ration* books with

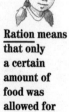

Ration means that only a certain amount of food was allowed for each person.

food stamps in them. They used the stamps
to buy food, gas, and clothes. If they ran
out of stamps for things like meat or but-
ter, they had to think of something else for
dinner.

Victory Gardens
Because vegetables were in short supply,
the government urged people to grow their
own. Many people turned their backyards

Annie and Jack's
Victory Garden

Forty percent of all vegetables in America came from these gardens.

into vegetable patches. Because the gardens were helping the war effort, people called them victory gardens. There were 20 million of them!

Women Go to Work

Factories ran night and day making weapons and other military equipment. Women who hadn't been allowed to work in factories before the war did jobs men had always done.

These women are riveting airplane parts. Rivets are pins that hold pieces of metal together.

They built airplanes. They also trained as pilots so they could deliver planes from one part of the country to another.

Women held jobs as welders, electricians, and riveters. They sewed uniforms, repaired machinery, and drove

Rosie the Riveter

Posters urging women to work were all over public spaces. Rosie the Riveter was a character from a government campaign.

trucks. And when they weren't working, many had to raise their children alone, since their husbands were in the war.

Women in the Military
There was no draft for women, and they weren't allowed to fight. However,

almost 400,000 volunteered to serve in the military.

Some women soldiers repaired vehicles and weapons. To free up male soldiers to fight, they also worked in war offices and as drivers or mail clerks.

Many faced danger, especially nurses who worked in hospitals near the fighting. Army nurses also served on ships and on planes carrying wounded soldiers to safety.

Some nurses were taken prisoner.

Two hundred and one nurses died in the war, some by enemy fire and others by accident or illness.

Japanese Internment Camps

Although people were united in the war effort, an unfair thing was happening to Japanese Americans.

Even though they were loyal Americans and many were fighting in the war, the government was afraid that some of them might support Japan or act as spies. President Roosevelt signed an order saying that Japanese Americans should be placed in *internment camps.*

In March 1942, 122,000 Japanese Americans from California, Oregon, and Washington had to leave their homes and businesses. They were ordered to report to one of ten internment camps around the country.

Internment camps are places where people are held against their will.

The camps had barbed-wire fences around them. People were not allowed to come and go as they pleased. Families lived in small rooms in barracks and lined up to use the bathroom and get their meals.

In spite of the hardships, Japanese Americans tried to keep their lives as normal as possible. Children went to school, and adults worked as teachers, doctors, and farmworkers.

It wasn't until 1945 that they were allowed to return to the homes they'd left almost three years before.

In 1988, Congress passed a law that said the camps were wrong. The U.S. government paid each person who had been in one to try to help make up for the unfairness.

British Kids During the Blitz

Life was scary for British kids living in a city during the Blitz. Their houses and schools could be bombed. They spent many nights in air-raid shelters with strangers. Families risked their lives every day.

To keep kids safe, the government sent thousands of them to live with strangers in the countryside. They had to pack their clothes and a gas mask to survive a possible gas attack. Then they said good-bye to their parents and friends. Some kids spent the whole war living far away from home.

5

Codes, Spies, and the Resistance

Have you ever written anything in code? Writing in code is a way to give secret information to someone.

In times of war, military leaders often send coded messages. George Washington used spies and sent coded messages during the Revolutionary War. The Axis and the Allies also had codes, and theirs were very hard to figure out.

When people write in code, they use numbers, letters, names, and special symbols that stand for words. The person getting the coded message knows what these things mean, but other people don't. They have to try to break the code.

The men and women who were code breakers in World War II were the kind of people who liked math, chess, and languages. Special groups of them worked together in England and the United States. The Allies decoded important German messages that helped them plan the D-Day invasion.

The Enigma Code

The Germans used a code called the Enigma code, which was created by an Enigma machine.

An **enigma** is a puzzle.

In 1941, the Allies captured a German U-boat that had an Enigma machine on board. Having the machine helped a group of top British code breakers solve the code.

Alan Turing was a math genius who was largely responsible for cracking the Enigma code.

Sending the Codes

Codes were often sent on military telephones by radio signals or on radio programs.

Another way to send codes was by war pigeons. Specially trained pigeons carried coded messages. Britain used about 250,000 of them.

The pigeons had a small tube with the message in it attached to one leg. They also had pouches that fit over their backs.

Pigeon handlers trained war pigeons to return to their nests. These nests were often near military bases.

Pilots would take the birds with them when they flew near enemy lines. They dropped them down to earth in little parachutes.

 This photo from 1940 shows British soldiers training a war pigeon.

People behind the lines got the pi-geons and attached messages to them about enemy movements. Then they would release the birds so they could fly back to the base in Britain.

The Romans used carrier pigeons 2,000 years ago.

Navajo Code Talkers

Not many people other than the Navajo (NAH-vuh-ho) know the Navajo language.

The marines chose 400 Navajo men to be "code talkers." They had to be able to speak both English and Navajo. It was their mission to send coded messages to each other using the Navajo language.

Because the Navajo language wasn't well known, the Japanese were never able to break their code.

Code talkers often used Navajo words

Navajo code talkers

to stand for English words. For example, the Navajo word for "turtle" meant tanks. "Potatoes" were grenades, and "whales" were battleships.

Iwo Jima is a small island in the Pacific. During World War II, it had two important Japanese airfields on it. Japanese planes based on the island often attacked U.S. planes on the way to Japan. The Americans needed to capture the island and use it for their planes.

During the Battle of Iwo Jima, six code talkers sent over 800 messages in the first two days of the battle. Their work helped American soldiers capture the island.

The United States Marine Corps War Memorial shows soldiers raising the American flag on Iwo Jima.

Members of the Italian Resistance

The Resistance

All over Europe, men and women risked their lives working for the Allies behind enemy lines. These brave people felt it was important to stand up for what was right, in spite of the danger. This underground movement was called the Resistance.

Many members of the Resistance worked as spies. They also *sabotaged*

Sabotage means to destroy or damage something.

(SAB-uh-tahjed) Axis bridges, railroads, telephone lines, and other things needed for the German war effort.

The Resistance worked in secret to hide Allied airmen who had been shot down behind enemy lines.

Spies also landed on the beaches in Japan. Some put rubber feet over their shoes—they looked like bare feet so the Japanese would think the prints were from fishermen!

The SOE

Early in the war, Winston Churchill created a secret organization called the Special Operations Executive (SOE).

The SOE trained people to work as Resistance fighters. They learned codes and how to use explosives. The SOE worked in almost all the countries occupied by the Axis.

Some brave men and women of the SOE parachuted behind enemy lines. Their courage helped keep the Axis from winning the war.

The White Mouse

Nancy Wake was one of the most famous SOE agents. Because she was so hard to catch, Nancy's nickname was the White Mouse.

Nancy was from New Zealand. She worked as a journalist in France and married a wealthy Frenchman.

When the Nazis invaded France, she carried messages for the French Resistance. When someone told the Nazis about her, Nancy had to

Nancy Wake

escape from France. After six tries, she finally got to Spain by hiding in the back of a coal truck.

Nancy went on to Britain, and once there, she joined the SOE.

Life in the SOE

In 1944, Nancy parachuted into France. She made it safely even though her parachute got tangled in a tree.

 Resistance forces destroy the railroad tracks connecting Marseille and Paris in 1944.

Nancy organized 7,500 people to work alone or in small groups to destroy factories, railroads, and bridges. This made

98

it hard for the Germans to get supplies when they needed them.

Shortly before D-Day, Nancy rode a bike 250 miles through German lines to contact the Allies. The trip took seventy-two hours!

Nancy once led a raid on a Nazi head-quarters in Montluçon, France, that killed thirty-eight Nazis. She and her people ambushed German trucks and supplied weapons to Resistance fighters who had parachuted into France.

After the war, Britain and the United States awarded medals to Nancy for her heroism. France gave her its highest military award, the Legion of Honor.

Nancy lived to be ninety-eight years old. She once said, "I was never afraid. I was too busy to be afraid."

Nancy received more medals than any other woman in the war.

Things You'd Need

If you were in the SOE, you might need:

a pencil with a dagger in it

shoes with hidden blades

a camera that fit in a matchbox

a radio that fit in a cookie tin

spikes to puncture tires

a compass that looked like a
button or piece of jewelry

קיינמאָל מער
PLUS JAMAIS
NEVER AGAIN
NIE WIEDER
НИКОГДА БОЛЬШЕ

6

The Holocaust

It is awful to imagine, but the Nazis wanted to get rid of anyone who did not fit their idea of what a perfect European should be. In addition to Jewish people, this included *Romani*, Slavs, handicapped people, and anyone who disagreed with what the Nazis were doing.

Romani are a nomadic people sometimes called gypsies.

Hitler began a terrible plan to deal with what he considered the problem of

Hitler Youth were young members of the Nazi party. By 1939, all German boys and girls were required to join.

Jewish people in Germany and the rest of Europe.

The Nazis urged men to sign up as Storm Troopers. They even expected children to be involved in their plans by joining the Hitler Youth.

On November 9, 1938, Nazi Storm

Troopers and members of the Hitler Youth in Germany and Austria rampaged through towns and cities. They burned and wrecked Jewish homes, synagogues, and businesses. As German policemen and crowds of people watched, they beat up or killed innocent people. There was so much damage that the day became known as *Kristallnacht* (KREES-tahl-noct), or the "night of the broken glass."

Ghettos

Whenever the Nazis invaded a country, they forced Jewish people in cities and towns to live in certain areas called ghettos.

The ghetto in Lodz, Poland

Barbed-wire fences and guards prevented anyone from leaving the ghetto. People were crammed together in small apartments. They couldn't stay warm in the winter, and many died from diseases and lack of food and medical care.

In 1942, the Nazis made a rule that Jews had to sew a yellow star on their clothes so everyone knew they were Jewish.

They were called <u>concentration camps</u> because people were concentrated, or grouped together, in one place.

Concentration Camps

After Kristallnacht, the Nazis began sending Jewish men, women, and children from ghettos and cities to *concentration camps*.

These Jewish men were forced onto trains leaving Paris in 1941.

108

The sign over the gate at the Auschwitz concentration camp means "Work sets you free."

Life in the concentration camps was a horror beyond belief. There was very little food. People were made to work until they dropped from exhaustion. Brutal prison guards often beat and even killed them.

Death Camps

The *Holocaust* (HAUL-uh-kost) is a term used for the murder of millions of people by the Nazis. In 1941 and 1942, the Nazis began opening camps that were built just for this purpose. The Nazis killed more than six million Jewish people and millions of others, including Slavs, Romani, and handicapped people, in the Holocaust.

After the war, some men and women who were guards in the camps were put on trial and punished.

In 1945, when the war was winding down, Allied armies marched into the death camps to free the survivors.

Most of the soldiers had seen brutal and bloody battles. But when they saw what the Nazis had done in the death camps, they wept.

Anne Frank

Anne Frank

Anne Frank was a Jewish girl who lived with her family in Amsterdam. When the Nazis started rounding up Jewish people,

Four heroic friends from his business risked their lives to keep the Franks hidden and safe.

the Frank family hid in secret rooms in the building where Anne's father worked.

The hideout had four tiny rooms and an attic. These rooms became home for Anne, her parents, and her sister. Later, four other Jewish people joined them.

During the day, everyone whispered and walked softly so that workers on the first floor wouldn't hear them and report them to the Nazis. They lived there for two years.

Anne's Diary

To pass the long, quiet days, Anne wrote in a diary. She wrote about small, everyday things. She also put down her feelings and hopes for the future. In her diary, Anne wrote, "In spite of everything, I still believe that people

are really good at heart."

Someone eventually told the Nazis about the Franks' hiding place. The Nazis arrested all of them and sent them to concentration camps. Sadly, Anne's father was the only one who survived.

After the war, he had Anne's diary published in Holland. Since then, millions of people have read and been moved by the young girl's words.

The Secret Room

Corrie ten Boom and her family lived above their watch repair shop in the Netherlands. Corrie's family had strong Christian beliefs and were willing to risk their lives to save others, especially Jewish people.

During the war, the ten Booms built a small secret room off Corrie's bedroom that was big enough to hide six people from the Nazis.

Some stayed for several days; others stayed for just a few hours, until a safe place could be found. During the war, the ten Boom family sheltered 800 Jewish people.

When someone revealed their secret, the Nazis sent the ten Boom family to concentration camps. Corrie's sister and

The house is now a museum, where visitors can see the secret room.

father died. Because there was a mistake in paperwork at the camp, Corrie was accidentally released early.

After the war, Corrie set up a refuge

for people recovering from the horror of what they'd seen. For the rest of her life, she traveled the world urging people to love and care for one another.

After the Holocaust

When the war was over, many Jewish people who had survived the Nazis left Europe. They settled in Canada, the United States, South America, and South Africa, among other places. More than 100,000 also went to live in the new state of Israel.

For thousands of years, many Jewish people had thought of this region in the Middle East as their homeland. The United Nations decided that after the Holocaust, Jewish people needed a land of their own. The UN voted to set aside land for the country that became Israel. More Jewish people live in Israel today than in any other place in the world.

On May 14, 1948, David Ben-Gurion, the first prime minister of Israel, announced the formation of the country.

Holocaust Survivors

Many survivors of the Holocaust wound up leading successful lives. Among these were famous musicians, writers, teachers, and businessmen.

Elie Wiesel

Elie Wiesel, for example, survived the camps as a child. He became a college teacher and wrote books about what he had experienced during the Holocaust. In 1986, Elie won the Nobel Peace Prize for his message of peace and healing.

Alice Herz-Sommer lived in a concentration camp and lost most of her family there. She was a great pianist who played in concerts all over the world. She kept playing until she was over one hundred years old! She lived until she was 110.

Alice Herz-Sommer

Alice once said, "Life is beautiful. You have to be thankful that we are living. Wherever you look is beauty. I know about the bad things, but I look for the good things."

7

The End of the War

Six weeks after landing in Normandy, the Allies marched into Paris. Thousands of happy people lined the streets to cheer their arrival.

The Allies' next goal was to reach Hitler's headquarters in Berlin, Germany.

As American, British, Canadians, and French soldiers were closing in from the west, Soviet troops were marching from the east.

ets surrounded Berlin. As
к over the city, Hitler hid in an
ground bunker. When he realized
ouldn't win, he killed himself. The
ermans knew it was all over and surrendered on May 7 and 8, 1945.

On May 8, people in the United States

Allied bombs destroyed much of Berlin.

and Great Britain and throughout Europe celebrated Victory in Europe Day, or V-E Day for short.

War Ends in Japan

President Roosevelt didn't live to see victory. He died in the spring of 1945, and the nation went into mourning. Harry Truman became the next president.

Truman's swearing-in

By June 1945, the Allies were closing in on Japan. They knew that if they invaded Japan, thousands of soldiers would die.

President Truman decided to drop an atomic bomb on the Japanese city of Hiroshima, hoping it would force Japan to surrender.

Atomic bomb over Nagasaki

The giant blast killed or wounded more than 180,000 people and destroyed the city.

Three days later, when the Japanese still hadn't given up, the Americans dropped a second bomb on the city of Nagasaki. Up to 80,000 people died in the first few days. But many more people in both cities died later from radiation sickness and injuries.

On August 15, 1945, the Japanese finally surrendered. The war was over.

Since 1942, scientists in America had been working in secret to make an atomic bomb. It was the most destructive bomb ever invented.

Colors, Fifth Avenue, Victory Parade 93-1

After World War II

After the war, there were trials in Germany and Japan for the men and women who had been responsible for so much horror. Eighteen Nazi war criminals received the death penalty or were sentenced to prison. General Tojo and six other Japanese officials were sentenced to death.

The Italians turned against Mussolini and killed him in 1945.

Today

Europe was so badly damaged during the war that the United States created a plan to help rebuild its cities and factories. It was called the Marshall Plan. The United States gave $13 billion to this cause.

In Japan, General MacArthur led U.S. forces that helped the country recover and become a democracy.

Today, the United States, Germany, and Japan support each other. And all over the world, there are memorials to Holocaust victims and to people who died in the war. These memorials remind us of the most terrible war in history so that it never happens again.

Doing More Research

There's a lot more you can learn about World War II. Find out how many different sources you can explore.

Books

Most libraries and bookstores have books about World War II.

Here are some things to remember when you're using books for research:

1. You don't have to read the whole book. Check the table of contents and the index to find the topics you're interested in.

2. Write down the name of the book.

When you take notes, make sure you write down the name of the book in your notebook so you can find it again.

3. Never copy exactly from a book.

When you learn something new from a book, put it in your own words.

4. Make sure the book is <u>nonfiction</u>.

Some books tell make-believe stories about World War II. Make-believe stories are called *fiction*. They're interesting to read, but not good for research.

Research books have facts and tell true stories. They are called *nonfiction*. A librarian or teacher can help you make sure the books you use for research are nonfiction.

Here are some good nonfiction books about World War II:

- *Franklin D. Roosevelt: A Leader in Troubled Times*, Time for Kids Biographies series, by the editors of *TIME for Kids* with Jeremy Caplan
- *Simple History: A Simple Guide to World War II* by Daniel Turner
- *True Stories of D-Day* by Henry Brook
- *What Was D-Day?* by Patricia Brennan Demuth
- *What Was Pearl Harbor?* by Patricia Brennan Demuth
- *Who Was Anne Frank?* by Ann Abramson
- *Who Was Franklin Roosevelt?* by Margaret Frith

- *Why Did the Whole World Go to War? And Other Questions About World War II*, Good Question! series, by Martin W. Sandler

- *World War II*, a DK Eyewitness book, by Simon Adams

- *You Wouldn't Want to Be a World War II Pilot!* by Ian Graham

Museums

Many museums can help you learn more about the Second World War.

When you go to a museum:

1. Be sure to take your notebook!
Write down anything that catches your interest. Draw pictures, too!

2. Ask questions.
There are almost always people at museums who can help you find what you're looking for.

3. Check the calendar.
Many museums have special events and activities just for kids!

Here are some museums with exhibits about World War II:

- National Infantry Museum & Soldier Center (Columbus, Georgia)
- National WWII Museum (New Orleans)
- Smithsonian WWII Aviation exhibit (Washington, D.C.)
- United States Holocaust Memorial Museum (Washington, D.C.)
- USS *Arizona* Memorial (Pearl Harbor, Hawaii)
- USS *Midway* Museum (San Diego)

The Internet

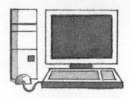

Many websites have lots of facts about World War II. Some also have activities that can help make learning about it easier.

Ask your teacher or your parents to help you find more websites like these:

- amhistory.si.edu/ourstory/activities /internment/index.html

- encyclopedia.kids.net.au/page/co /Codetalkers

- ducksters.com/history/world_war_ii

- history.com/topics/world-war-ii/anne -frank

- historylearningsite.co.uk/world-war-two /children-and-world-war-two

Index

Photographs courtesy of:

Have you read the adventure that matches up with this book? Don't miss

Magic Tree House®
SUPER EDITION #1

WORLD AT WAR, 1944

Jack and Annie go back in time to World War II and parachute behind enemy lines. Will they be able to make a difference during one of the darkest times in history?

Magic Tree House®

Magic Tree House® Merlin Missions

Magic Tree House®
Super Edition

#1: WORLD AT WAR, 1944

Magic Tree House®
Fact Trackers

More Magic Tree House®